Hot Spicy Trumpet Solos
with a Spanish Flair

by Gerald F. Knipfel

To access audio visit:
www.halleonard.com/mylibrary

Enter Code
4088-8543-5069-6144

ISBN 978-1-57424-388-8
SAN 683-8022

Special thanks to Kevin Delaney for the cover art. To David Hall for the Audio files and to Cameron Bradley for the music notation

Channel Note: On the Audio files the trumpet part will be on the left channel and Piano on the right channel

Copyright © 2020 CENTERSTREAM Publishing
P.O. Box 17878 - Anaheim Hills, CA 92817

www.centerstream-usa.com | centerstrm@aol.com | 714-779-9390

Table of Contents

Trumpet in B♭

EL FANDANGO
B♭ Trumpet Solo

Gerald Knipfel

Piano

EL FANDANGO
Piano Accompaniment

Gerald Knipfel

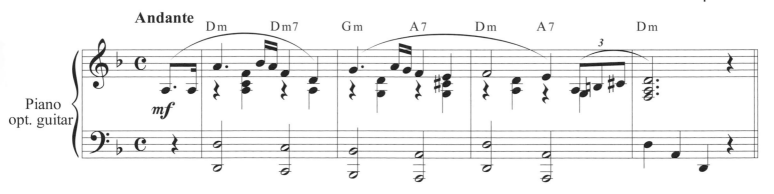

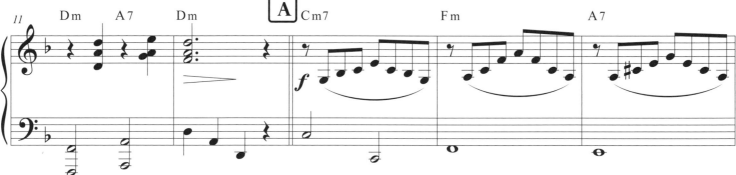

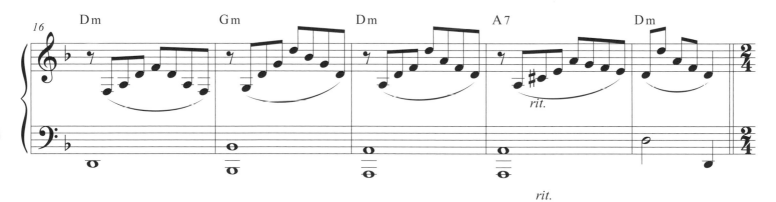

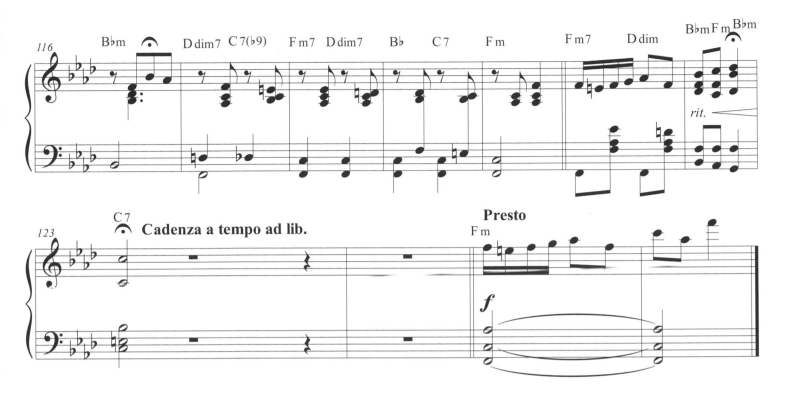

Score

EL FANDANGO
Full Score

Gerald Knipfel

11

12

13

15

EL VAQUERO
Bb Trumpet Solo with Piano Accompaniment

Trumpet in B♭

By Gerald Knipfel

17

EL VAQUERO
Piano Accompaniment

Piano

By Gerald Knipfel

EL VAQUERO
Full Score

Score

By Gerald Knipfel

MEXICANA
Bb Trumpet Solo

Gerald Knipfel

Piano

MEXICANA
Piano Accompaniment

By Gerald Knipfel

MEXICANA
Full Score

Score

By Gerald Knipfel

SONORA

Bb Trumpet Solo

Trumpet in B♭

Gerald Knipfel

SONORA
Piano Accompaniment

Piano

Gerald Knipfel

43

SONORA
Full Score

Score

Gerald Knipfel

45

Rafael Méndez Biography

Rafael Méndez (March 26, 1906 – September 15, 1981) was a Mexican virtuoso solo trumpeter. He is known as the "Heifetz of the Trumpet."

Méndez emigrated to the US, first settling in Gary, Indiana, at age 20 and worked in steel mills. He moved to Flint, Michigan and worked at a Buick automotive plant as he established his musical career.

From 1950 to 1975, Méndez was a full-time soloist. At the peak of his musicial career he performed about 125 concerts a year. He was also very active as a recording artist. By 1940, he was in Hollywood, leading the brass section of M-G-M's studio orchestra. He contributed to the films *Flying Down to Rio* and *Hondo*, among others.

Méndez was legendary for his tone, range, technique and unparalleled double tonguing. His playing was characterized by a brilliant tone, wide vibrato and clean, rapid articulation. His repertoire was a mixture of classical, popular, jazz, and Mexican folk music. He contributed many arrangements and original compositions to the trumpet repertoire. His "Scherzo in D Minor" is often heard in recitals, and has been recorded by the world's pre-eminent trumpet virtuoso, David Hickman.

Méndez is regarded as popularizing "La Virgen de la Macarena," commonly known as "the bullfighter's song," to US audiences. Perhaps his most significant if not famous single recording, "Moto Perpetuo", was written in the eighteenth century by Niccolò Paganini for violin and features Méndez double-tonguing continuously for over 4 minutes while circular breathing to give the illusion that he is not taking a natural breath while playing.

Arizona State University's music building houses the 1,400 sq ft Rafael Méndez Library which was dedicated and opened on June 11, 1993. The library holds 300 manuscripts and almost 700 compositions and arrangements by Méndez, as well as hundreds of images, articles and recordings. It also has an online counterpart.

In 2006, the Los Angeles Opera paid tribute to Rafael Méndez by performing a work based on his life. A reviewer in The Los Angeles Times believed that Méndez "has been called the greatest trumpet player of all time."